GEOGRAPHY FACT FILES

COASTLINES

· ·

Michael Kerrigan

A⁺
Smart Apple Media

GEOGRAPHY FACT FILES

COASTLINES
DESERTS
MOUNTAINS
OCEANS
POLAR REGIONS
RIVERS

First published in 2004 by Hodder Wayland
338 Euston Road, London NW1 3BH, United Kingdom
Hodder Wayland is an imprint of Hodder Children's
Books, a division of Hodder Headline Limited. This
edition published under license from Hodder Children's
Books. All rights reserved.

Produced for Hodder Wayland by
Monkey Puzzle Media Ltd
Gissing's Farm, Fressingfield, Suffolk IP21 5SH
United Kingdom
Copyright © 2004 Hodder Wayland

Editor	Paul Mason
Designer	Mark Whitchurch
Picture Researcher	Sally Cole
Illustrator	Michael Posen
Consultant	Michael Allaby

Published in the United States by Smart Apple Media
2140 Howard Drive West
North Mankato, Minnesota 56003

U.S. publication copyright © 2005 Smart Apple Media
International copyright reserved in all countries. No part
of this book may be reproduced in any form without
written permission from the publisher.
Printed in China

Library of Congress Cataloging-in-Publication Data

Kerrigan, Michael.
Coastlines / Michael Kerrigan.
p. cm. — (Geography fact files)
Includes bibliographical references
ISBN 1-58340-424-4

1. Coasts—Juvenile literature. I. Title. II. Series.

GB453.K47 2004

551.45'7—dc22 2004042920

9 8 7 6 5 4 3 2 1

Acknowledgements
We are grateful to the following for permission to
reproduce photographs: A1 Pix 3 top (Superbild), 3
middle (Claes Axstal/Superbild), 11 (Superbild), 16 (Claes
Axstal/Superbild), 36 (Superbild); Alamy back cover left
(Bryan and Cherry Alexander), 5 bottom (ImageState/
Pictor International), 9 bottom (Buzz Pictures), 13 top
(Chris Gomersall), 15 top (Doug Steley), 23 bottom
(Robert Harding Picture Library), 28 (Bryan and Cherry
Alexander), 29 (Steven Allan); Corbis 6 (Jonathan Blair),
8 (Bettmann), 10 (James L Amos), 17 (Michael Busselle),
20 (Jason Hawkes), 21 top (NASA), 31 (Lowell Georgia),
32 (Tiziana and Gianni Baldizzone), 34 (Bill Ross), 37
(Dave Bartruff), 45 top (Philip Wallick); Eye Ubiquitous
1 (Tim Hawkins), 19 bottom (Tim Hawkins); FLPA 5 top
(D Fleetham/Silvestris), 25 bottom (T Fitzharris/Minden
Pictures), 26 (E and D Hosking); Hutchison Library 3
bottom (Bernard Regent), 18 (Bernard Regent), 40
(Bernard Regent); James Davis Worldwide 33 (James
Davis), 42, 43 top; PA Photos 41 (EPA), 43 bottom (EPA);
Nature Picture Library 7 (Rick Price), 12 (Michael Pitts), 24
(Tony Heald), 27 (Tony Heald); Photodisc Collection front
cover (Getty Images); Rex Features 4 (Richard Austin), 30
bottom (David Lane/PBP); Science Photo Library 13
bottom (NASA), 25 top (Dr Gene Feldman/NASA GSFC);
Still Pictures 15 bottom (Nigel Dickinson), 21 bottom
(Fred Bavendam), 22 (Bojan Brecelj), 35 (Reinhard Janke),
38 right (Mark Edwards), 38 left (Hartmut Schwarzbach),
44–45 (Schalharijk/UNEP), 45 bottom (Hartmut
Schwarzbach), 47 (Bojan Brecelj).

Title page picture: Waves break against the rocky coast
of southern England's Portland Bill.

CONTENTS

Introduction   4
How the coasts were formed   6
Waves   8
Tides   10
Currents   12
Coastal weather patterns   14
The seashore   16
Erosion   18
Deposition   20
Salt marshes and deltas   22
Aquatic animals   24
A variety of birds   26
A home for humans   28
Coastal management   30
The kindly coast   32
Trade   34
Coastal navigation   36
Fishing   38
Seaside tourism   40
A fragile environment   42
A world awash?   44
Glossary   46
Further information   47
Index   48

INTRODUCTION

The coastline is the point at which the sea meets the land: the confrontation between the two is what creates and shapes the coasts. Sea and land may react with one another in many different ways, so the result is a complex environment—and a very varied one.

A STATE OF CHANGE

Coastlines are constantly changing. Each day their outline is altered as the tides rise and fall. Other transformations take place more slowly, over thousands of years. **Plates** of rock may be raised up or dashed down by the action of earthquakes and volcanoes; jagged outcrops or smooth shorelines may be formed. Pounding waves wear away the land at one point, then pile up debris—new land—at another. Winds scoop up sand and heap it into drifting dunes. Rivers lay down **sediment** as they reach the sea, which may form salt marshes or **mangrove** swamps.

FACT FILE

COASTLINE LENGTHS

A comparison between the coastline lengths of continents and countries can produce some surprising results. Look at Norway, for instance, against the much-bigger United States:

World	527,000 miles (850,000 km)
Asia	38,936 miles (62,800 km)
Europe	23,560 miles (38,000 km)
Australia	15,971 miles (25,760 km)
Canada	151,150 miles (243,791 km)
Norway	13,594 miles (21,925 km)
United States	12,353 miles (19,924 km)
United Kingdom	7,706 miles (12,429 km)
Denmark	4,535 miles (7,314 km)

Giant waves lash England's Dorset coast, threatening life and property. The sea is destructive, but it can also create new land.

The clear waters of this Indonesian coral reef are an ecological wonderland—and a diver's paradise.

NATURAL WONDERS

Every natural coastline is an astonishing **ecosystem** in itself, with its own unique diversity of species, from seaweeds to birds, from **mollusks** to mammals. In warm water, coral reefs may flourish. These are home to some of the world's most exotic and colorful marine animals. The rock pools of cooler coasts can also contain a variety of different creatures.

A HOME FOR HUMANS

The coast is a crucial element in the human environment, too. The sea is an important source of food and a highway for trade. But the sea has also been a convenient dumping-ground for sewage and industrial waste. Many coastlines are badly polluted; sometimes the sea is not even healthy to swim in.

Sun, sea, and sand—an irresistible combination for visitors like these at California's Venice Beach.

FACT FILE

HOW FAR PEOPLE LIVE FROM THE SEA WORLDWIDE

DISTANCE FROM SEA	PERCENTAGE OF POPULATION
less than 19 miles (30 km)	20.6
19–37 miles (30-60 km)	8.6
37–56 miles (60-90 km)	5.8
56–74 miles (90-120 km)	4.5
greater than 74 miles (120 km)	60.5

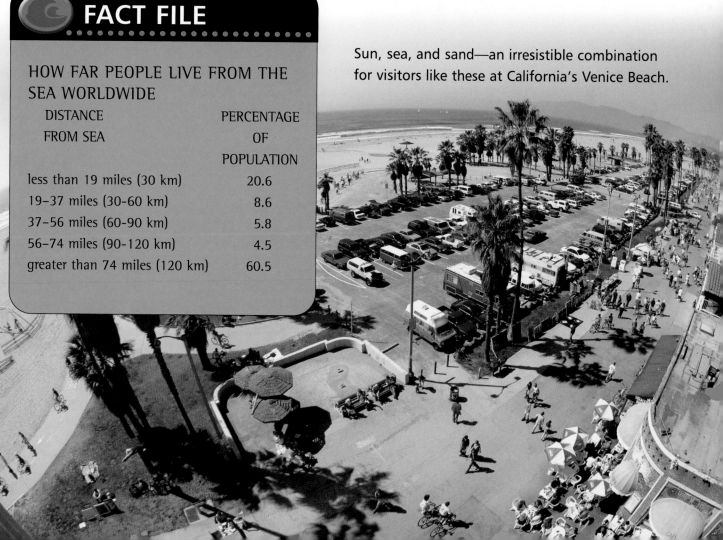

HOW THE COASTS WERE FORMED

The extreme forces that built the world have left their record along the coastlines. Those who know what to look for can see evidence of the violence of the continents' first formation, earthquakes and volcanoes, and great glaciations.

A WORLD ADRIFT

Around 250 million years ago, a single sea surrounded one vast supercontinent, now known as Pangea. Around 200 million years ago, this landmass began to disintegrate. Pangea was riding like a raft on an ocean of super-hot rock, or **magma**, some 40 to 60 miles (70–100 km) below.

As magma pushed up through cracks in the rock, Pangea was broken into separate sections, or plates. At fractions of an inch per year, the process was very slow, but it never stopped. Between 100 and 50 million years ago, the different continents people know today were largely formed. Tremors and volcanic eruptions accompanied this violent break-up of Earth's land surface, throwing up headlands in one place, and dragging down sections of coastline in another. The continents continue their slow drift today.

Over the centuries, the coast at Pozzuoli has been forced up and down: at one time these ruins were underwater.

LOCATION FILE

POZZUOLI'S UPS AND DOWNS

The Roman Temple of Serapis, in Pozzuoli, Italy, is as interesting to geologists as to archaeologists. Around the bases of its columns are the tiny boreholes of marine mollusks. Built on dry land, the site must have spent several centuries under water, before continued **seismic** activity forced this coastline up again.

THE EARTH TAKES SHAPE

- **4,550 MYA (MILLION YEARS AGO)**
The solar system takes form out of the debris of a dying star.
- **3,500 MYA** The first life: **microorganisms** appear on Earth.
- **200 MYA** The dinosaurs appear; the break-up of Pangea begins.
- **4 MYA** The first **hominids** (humanlike creatures) appear.
- **2 MYA** The ice age begins.
- **100,000 YA (YEARS AGO) Homo sapiens**—modern humans—appear.
- **11,000 YA** The last glaciation ends.

THE EARTH UNDER ICE

Climatic changes affected the physical forms of the continents. Most dramatic were the ice ages of the past two million years. Today's polar ice caps are what remains of the last glaciation—which reached its greatest extent only 20,000 years ago. Ice sheets miles thick crept across the continents, clearing empty plains and gouging out deep valleys. The sheer weight of ice pushed the land surface down in many areas. The effects of the freeze on sea levels was still more striking. Much of Earth's moisture was locked up in the ice, causing the waters at first to retreat and then, when the thaw came, to rise again abruptly. All these actions affected the shape of the world's coasts.

Snow and ice like that found today in Antarctica once covered much of the planet.

WAVES

The sea is never still: even on windless days its surface is disturbed by waves, which lap gently or roll as breakers onto sandy or rocky shores. These waves may have traveled hundreds of miles from the storms that first created them.

WAVE FORMATION

Waves are caused by winds as they brush against the surface of the sea. As energy is transferred from air to water, ripples form—the faster the wind, the more energy is transferred and the bigger the waves. Wave size also varies according to the distance over which the wind has been blowing. Larger waves build up only in great, wide oceans; in smaller seas, such as the Mediterranean, average wave height is much lower. Waves are a **transmission** of energy, not a movement of water. Just watch a floating bottle as it bobs up on a passing wave: once the wave has passed, the bottle drops down again exactly where it was before, rather than being moved along by the water.

Although it originated in the Caribbean, Hurricane Carol ravaged the entire eastern seaboard of America in August 1954. Here, a man clings to a tree for support in Brooklyn, New York City.

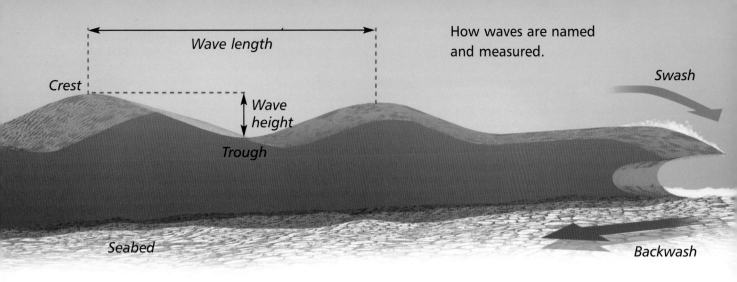

Wave length

Crest

Wave height

Trough

Seabed

How waves are named and measured.

Swash

Backwash

WHEN WAVES REACH THE SHORE

In shallow water, a wave's energy is reduced by contact with the seabed below. The base slows while the crest (top) continues at the same speed: the wave "breaks," tumbling forward as though tripping over itself.

Along irregular coastlines, waves hit the shallows at all sorts of odd angles, so the seabed drags at the wave sooner at one point than another. With one side held back while the other rushes on unhindered, the entire wave changes direction. This phenomenon is known as wave refraction.

TSUNAMIS

A tsunami is a wave that takes its energy not from the wind but from seismic activity: a volcanic eruption or earthquake, for example. In deep water they may pass almost unnoticed. When they reach coastal shallows, however, they rise to terrifying heights. A big tsunami may wreak havoc far inland.

FACT FILE

MAJOR MODERN TSUNAMIS, WITH
APPROXIMATE NUMBER OF CASUALTIES
- LISBON, PORTUGAL, 1755   60,000
- SUNDA STRAIT, INDONESIA, 1883
(after Krakatoa eruption)   36,400
- CHILE, 1960   2,000
- MORO GULF, PHILIPPINES, 1976   10,000
- FLORES, INDONESIA, 1992   1,700

Below: Unhindered by rocks and headlands, and raised up steadily by a gently rising beach, these waves march in with great precision.

TIDES

T o ancient peoples, the tides were mysterious events. Twice each day the level of the ocean would rise and fall, in some places by large distances. Today, scientists have confirmed that the tides are mainly caused by the gravitational attraction of the moon.

THE MOON'S EFFECT

Every heavenly body has its own field of gravity. The bigger it is, the stronger its **gravitational force**. The pull of the moon is felt on Earth mainly in the effect it has on the level of the seas. As it circles Earth, the moon's gravity gently pulls the waters of the seas and oceans toward it. A "bulge" of water follows the moon's passage across the surface of the seas, with another bulge on the other side of the planet. The result is called tides: the rising (flow) and falling (ebb) of water levels. Since the moon's movements are predictable, so too are tidal patterns.

FACT FILE

TIDAL RANGES AROUND THE WORLD

A tidal range is the difference between water levels at high tide and at low tide in a particular location. Tidal range can vary dramatically from place to place:

- Bay of Fundy, eastern Canada: 52 feet (16 m)
- Avonmouth, England: 49 feet (15 m)
- Seattle, Washington: 11 feet (3.4 m)
- La Coruña, Spain: 9.5 feet (2.9 m)
- Lowestoft, England: 6.2 feet (1.9 m)
- Galveston, Texas: 2 feet (0.6 m)

A dry low-tide harbor testifies to the tidal range in the Channel Islands, UK.

COMPLICATIONS

Especially high tides are created when the moon is directly between the sun and Earth. The sun's gravitational pull is added to the moon's, and the tidal bulge of water increases in height. The smallest tides occur when Earth is directly between the sun and moon. The highest tides are known as spring tides; the lowest are neap tides.

If the globe were completely covered by ocean, the moon's effect would be the same worldwide, but some seas contain only small bodies of water, on which the moon has less effect. The Mediterranean, for example, scarcely has any tides at all, while the Gulf of Mexico has only one daily cycle instead of the usual two.

PEOPLE FILE

KING CANUTE

An 11th-century English king of Danish descent, Canute (or Knud) eventually wearied of his attendants' ceaseless flatteries. Told his greatness was such that he could even command the sea, he had his throne set up on the nearest shore. As the incoming tide rose higher, Canute ordered the waves to retreat: they ignored him and gave the courtiers' feet a thorough soaking.

Hydroelectricity, some of it generated by the ebb and flow of the tides, is an important source of energy. Water captured at high tide drives electrical turbines as it flows back toward the sea.

CURRENTS

A long with the daily back-and-forth of the tides and the lashing of wind-blown waves, less obvious movements of water influence the coastlines. The oceans are complex, dynamic systems full of energy, through which currents may circulate over thousands of miles.

THE GULF STREAM

The Gulf Stream is one of the world's great ocean currents. It is a flow of warm water from the Gulf of Mexico to the colder North Atlantic. It brings mild, moist weather to what might otherwise be a much colder British Isles. The Gulf Stream, like most ocean currents, is largely driven by winds.

WARM AND COLD CURRENTS

Ocean surface currents are driven by the wind. Warm **equatorial** waters are driven westward by winds blowing from the east. As these warm currents come close to continents they are deflected, and the **Coriolis effect** moves them to the right in the northern hemisphere and to the left in the southern hemisphere.

Sardines mass in their millions off the coast of Natal, South Africa.

LOCATION FILE

THE GREATEST SHOAL ON EARTH

Warm and cold currents collide off Ilovo Beach, South Africa, where the Agulhas Current meets the cold Benguela Stream. The result is an upwelling of water from the ocean floor that brings nutrients from the seabed. So eagerly do sardines take to the rich micro-life this upwelling sustains that they swarm here in staggering numbers every winter. Many fish thrash their way ashore in the crowding and confusion.

In the mid-**latitudes**, winds blow from the west. As the ocean currents enter this region, they are again turned in their course, to flow from west to east. As they hit the opposite continent from the one they first encountered, currents change course once again, this time turning back toward the equator. Eventually their waters rejoin the westward flow of equatorial currents.

At the same time, a current called the Great Conveyor carries cold water from the Arctic south along the Atlantic Ocean floor. The Conveyor eventually joins the eastward-flowing Antarctic Current, sending cold water into the Indian, Atlantic, and Pacific Oceans. Finally, it reaches Greenland, in the North Atlantic, by which time it has become a warm-water surface current.

A puffin perches amid grass and sea pink in Scotland's Treshnish Isles—where the local climate and ecology are heavily affected by the Gulf Stream.

The world's major ocean currents, as indicated by differences in sea-surface heights. These differences highlight major ocean currents (yellow, red, and white) in contrast with areas of stable sea surface (dark blue).

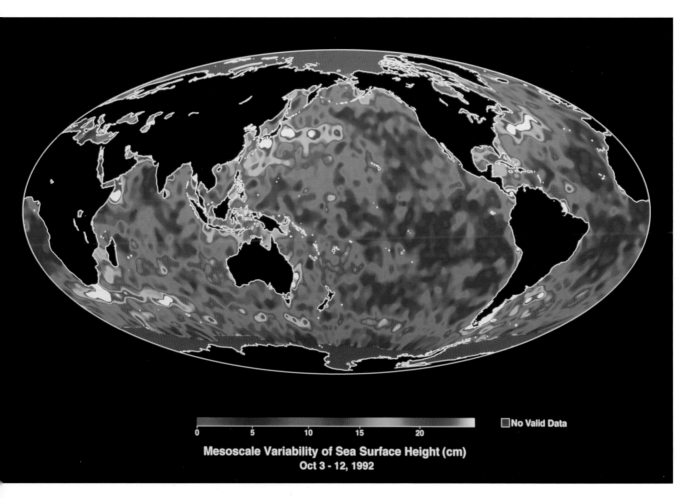

☐ No Valid Data

0   5   10   15   20

Mesoscale Variability of Sea Surface Height (cm)
Oct 3 - 12, 1992

COASTAL WEATHER PATTERNS

Walking along an exposed cliff top on a chilly, windy winter's day, one might imagine that the coast is the coldest place on Earth. The reality, in fact, is that the sea tends to have a moderating influence on climate, so coastal areas are often warmer than inland ones.

OCEANIC INSULATION

Water has a higher heat capacity than solid rock or earth: more heat is needed to achieve the same rise in temperature. But at the same time, water gives up the heat it has less easily, cooling more slowly once the heat source is removed. The sea thus acts as an insulating blanket for coastal areas, ensuring they're spared the worst extremes of temperature. This contrasts to the baking summers and frozen winters of the midwestern U.S. or Central Asia, which are too far from the ocean to be affected by its temperature.

SEA BREEZES

The difference in heat capacity between land and sea also has an impact at the local level. The temperature of the land rises more rapidly, and the air in contact with it is also warmed. The warm air becomes less dense, so the land's air can rise. Cooler air flows in from above the sea to replace it. This is warmed in its turn, and so the process continues in what is known as a **convection** current. This current creates a breeze from the sea to the land.

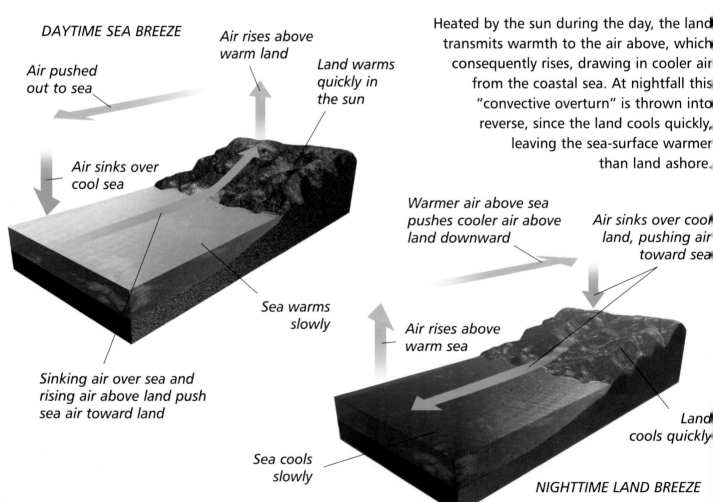

DAYTIME SEA BREEZE

Air pushed out to sea

Air rises above warm land

Land warms quickly in the sun

Air sinks over cool sea

Sea warms slowly

Sinking air over sea and rising air above land push sea air toward land

Heated by the sun during the day, the land transmits warmth to the air above, which consequently rises, drawing in cooler air from the coastal sea. At nightfall this "convective overturn" is thrown into reverse, since the land cools quickly, leaving the sea-surface warmer than land ashore.

Warmer air above sea pushes cooler air above land downward

Air sinks over cool land, pushing air toward sea

Air rises above warm sea

Sea cools slowly

Land cools quickly

NIGHTTIME LAND BREEZE

With the wave held up and made steeper by offshore winds, a surfer is able to build up amazing speeds on the wall of water.

STORMS

In tropical areas, where heat is intense, very strong convection currents may be established over open sea, sucking air into a moving spiral that then sweeps landward as a storm, gathering energy and violence as it goes. Such tropical storms may cause major devastation and loss of life. When sustained wind speeds exceed 74 miles (119 km) per hour, tropical storms are reclassified as tropical **cyclones**.

FACT FILE

AVERAGE TEMPERATURE HIGHS AND LOWS IN INLAND AND COASTAL CITIES

	COLDEST MONTH	WARMEST MONTH
Winnipeg (Canada, inland)	-2 °F (-19 °C)	68 °F (20 °C)
Seattle (U.S., coastal)	45 °F (7 °C)	66 °F (19 °C)
London (UK, coastal)	41 °F (5 °C)	64 °F (18 °C)
Moscow (Russia, inland)	14 °F (-10 °C)	66 °F (19 °C)

LOCATION FILE

HONDURAS MEETS HURRICANE MITCH

Hurricane Mitch hit Central America's Caribbean coast in autumn 1998, causing devastation. While terrifying winds blew down buildings and power lines, torrential rains caused floods and landslides. Crammed together on unstable hillsides, the flimsy shacks of the poor were especially vulnerable: more than 11,000 people died in Honduras and neighboring Nicaragua.

A young boy stands amid the wreckage of people's homes, which have been destroyed by the high winds of Hurricane Mitch.

THE SEASHORE

For many people, their first experience of the coast is a day out on a sandy beach. In sunny weather, when the sea is warm, the seaside is very enjoyable. But the sea can also be rough and cold. The coast itself is formed partly by the ocean's more violent conditions.

PULVERIZED

Every grain of sand tells a story of destruction: sand is made up of shattered crystals of minerals and the crushed remains of seashells. The process of making sand begins as debris is carried up and down in the swash (movement up the beach) and backwash (movement down) of the waves. Over time, larger fragments are worn smooth. Smaller stones are milled down to sand.

A raised bump, or berm, appears where sand accumulates at the high-tide line. As years pass, and the sea piles up more sand, the seaward edge of this moves forward, so that an area of sand is left high and dry behind. This is known as the backshore, while the area the sea still covers at high tide is the foreshore.

These defensive barriers at Skagen, Denmark, make the beach look odd, but they prevent the whole coast from being carried away by the waves.

FACT FILE

SAND
Sand is basically the ground-down, grainy residue of whatever rocks and minerals may be at hand, but quartz and feldspar are frequently present. The black beaches of Hawaii and several other Pacific Islands are formed from basaltic sand—crushed volcanic lava; a stark contrast with the shimmering white beaches to be seen elsewhere in the region, whose sand is composed of countless millions of minute fragments of coral.

THE DUNES OF JUTLAND

The North Sea coast of Jutland, Denmark, is a unique coastal environment, where windblown sand has rippled up rolling hills, or dunes. Nearest the sea are mobile dunes, which move along like super-slow-motion waves. Further inland are fixed dunes, grassed over, and marshy hollows, or slacks, where rare plant and animal species are found, including the natterjack toad.

PEBBLE BEACHES

Pebble beaches behave differently from sandy areas. With larger lumps of rock, there are bigger gaps through which water can flow. Although the swash throws debris up the beach, the backwash tends simply to trickle through. So a pebble beach is generally much steeper than a typical sandy one.

LONGSHORE DRIFT

Where waves approach a coast at an angle, they throw debris up the beach at a diagonal. Rather than retrace that precise path, however, the backwash tends to be drawn straight down the slope of the beach by gravity, leaving sediment slightly to one side of where it was before. The next wave carries it back up the beach once again at an angle, before its backwash runs straight down. Wave by wave the sediment is slowly moved along the beach in a zig-zag course. This is what causes longshore drift, the gradual sideways movement of the beach— so much so it may eventually be washed away completely.

Hauled safely above the high-water mark, fishing boats line the pebble beach at Hastings, on England's southern coast.

EROSION

During autumn, winter, and spring, the coasts are regularly battered by storms. These wear away at the coast in a process known as erosion. Every year, the forces of erosion break off bits of land; elsewhere, dramatic landforms are created by its actions.

One of the most important functions of a beach is to serve as a shock-absorber, protecting a coastline against the violence of the sea. A lot of energy is contained in a wave, and when it strikes land, that force has to go somewhere: on a beach it expends itself by moving sand and pebbles. Where that protection is absent, coasts bear the full force of every impact. Inevitably, they are worn down—eroded—by slow degrees. Where cliffs and headlands are made of softer rocks such as chalk or boulder clay, whole sections of coastline may crumble away in a single storm. Other coasts are eroded, too: more slowly, perhaps, but in the long run just as surely.

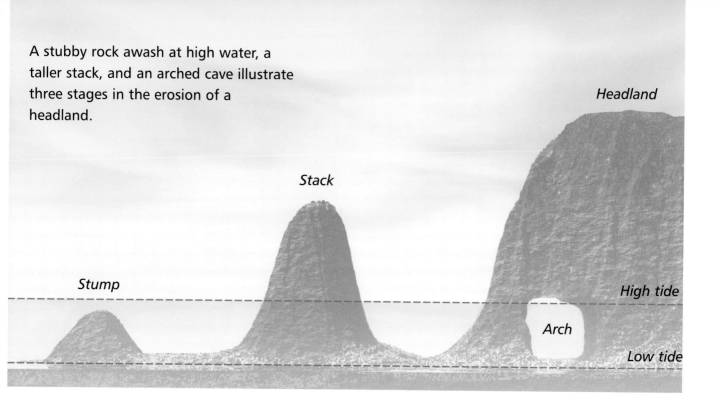

A stubby rock awash at high water, a taller stack, and an arched cave illustrate three stages in the erosion of a headland.

Headland

Stack

Stump

High tide

Arch

Low tide

SHAPING THE COASTS

Erosion may be a destructive force, but it has helped create today's coasts, giving them their distinctive forms and individual outlines. Where bands of hard and soft rock lie side by side, they wear away at different rates. This gives rise to irregularities such as headlands and bays, which are then increased by the effects of wave refraction (see page 9).

SEA SCULPTURES

On some rocky coasts, striking shapes are created by erosion. For example, waves scoop out hollows in the sides of headlands. In time, deep caves are created, or even arches that go right through. When the roofs of these collapse, free-standing towers, or stacks, are formed.

The sheer power of the waves as they pound against a rocky coast can be seen in this view of Portland Bill, on the southern coast of England.

FACT FILE

HOW WAVES CAUSE EROSION
• The sheer impact of the waves themselves.
• The impact of rocks or debris thrown by the waves (abrasion).
• **Hydraulic** pressure: water in cracks or chinks is squeezed when a big wave strikes, exerting stresses on the rock face from within.

DEPOSITION

The sea can be a destructive force, but it is also creative. Through deposition (the depositing, or putting down, of sand and mud) it builds up certain areas of coastline. Often the materials involved are actually the products of erosion elsewhere, the two processes balancing out over the longer term.

SPITS AND BARS

What is worn away in one place is liable to be washed up in another because of a lateral (along-the-beach) movement of sand or pebbles called longshore drift. Where the line of the coast cuts away abruptly inward, the drift continues in the same direction as before. It drops its load of sand or pebbles, slowly building up a barrier, or spit, protruding at an angle. This may grow so long that it cuts right across the mouth of a bay. Chesil Beach, a spit of this kind, effectively straightens out 19 miles (30 km) of southern English coastline.

Spits also form where the drift is obstructed by interference from a rival current—a river mouth, for example. As it hits the flow of water out of the mouth of a river, the longshore drift slackens and stalls, dumping its load to form a spit.

So straight it looks more like an artificial construction than a work of nature, southern England's Chesil Beach was formed by centuries of deposition.

BARRIER ISLANDS

Over time, spits can grow so much that barrier islands form. Flat, low-lying scraps of land, these rise above all but the highest, storm-assisted tides. Their soils are sandy but able to support hardy vegetation. Barrier islands can be found down much of the eastern coast of the U.S.

Cape Hatteras, in North Carolina, seen here from space, is fringed by a line of barrier islands.

LOCATION FILE

THE WADDEN ZEE
A chain of 23 barrier islands and connecting sandbars runs along the North Sea coasts of the Netherlands, Germany, and southern Denmark, marking off a huge lagoon that is known as the Wadden Zee. This separate, shallow sea, covering more than 4,290 square miles (11,000 sq km) at high tide, is fringed by an additional 136 square miles (350 sq km) of salt marsh and farmland.

CORAL REEFS

The reefs that skirt many warm-water coasts are formed from the hard outer skeletons of tiny creatures. As generations of corals reproduce and die, their skeletons cluster on top of one another, layer after layer: eventually, gigantic undersea structures may be formed.

LOCATION FILE

THE GREAT BARRIER REEF
Extending more than 1,240 miles (2,000 km) up the coast of Queensland, northeastern Australia, the Great Barrier Reef is one of the undisputed wonders of the natural world. It is not, in fact, a single reef but a chain of almost 3,000. It boasts 400 distinct types of coral, 1,500 fish species, and an amazing 4,000 different mollusks.

Chromis fish flit through a forest of corals on Australia's Great Barrier Reef.

SALT MARSHES AND DELTAS

Once a river reaches sea level, its waters are no longer forced toward the sea by gravity. Momentum spent, the river dumps whatever silt (mineral particles) it has been carrying. At the river's mouth, chemical reactions between fresh and salty water cause fine solid particles to stick together (flocculate) into heavier lumps. Here, large mudflats develop, providing a rich feeding-ground for birds.

SALT MARSHES

Neither land nor sea, salt marshes are a unique environment. Few plants can tolerate the fluctuating water levels there. On top of this, they are regularly doused in brine (salty water). For those hardy enough to withstand such treatment, though, there are real compensations: rich soils and fresh nutrients brought in with every tide.

Mangroves thrive in conditions that would kill other plant species. Their roots screen out salts, while pores above the waterline allow them to "breathe."

SPECIALIZED PLANTS

A range of specialized plants and shrubs has evolved to cope with these conditions. They either have glands that secrete out excess salt or have cells that store up water to dilute it to safe levels. While shrubs such as sea buckthorn can tolerate only occasional flooding, some sea grasses can cope with being covered twice daily, 365 days a year. Mangroves are full-sized trees that grow in tropical salt marshes: a weird and wonderful ecosystem has grown up around them, complete with tree-climbing crabs, mudskipper fish, aquatic monkeys, and other eccentric creatures.

THE MISSISSIPPI DELTA

The Mississippi Delta covers about one-quarter of the entire area of Louisiana: more than 12,870 square miles (33,000 sq km) in all. Its rich soils make its more inland areas perfect for growing fruit, vegetables, and other crops, though there are difficulties of access across a marshy landscape crisscrossed with creeks. As continuing silt deposits have gradually raised land levels across the delta, many former offshoots of the river have been cut off at either end, and now stand stagnant. These bayous are one of the Mississippi Delta's most distinctive features, supporting a rich and varied ecology all their own.

A typical "bird's foot" delta (above left), such as the Mississippi Delta (above right).

A typical "cuspate" delta (below left), such as the Ganges Delta (below right).

DELTAS

If enough sediment accumulates at a river mouth, it can end up extending the coastline and pushing back the sea. This process is known as progradation. With no valley walls to hold it back, the river tends to fan out into a lot of little channels. The result is a delta—so-called from the ancient Greek letter, which had the same triangular shape.

Mineral deposits enrich the soils of the Yellow River valley in China.

THE WORLD'S MUDDIEST RIVERS

Rivers are ranked by concentration of sediment in the water, not sheer quantity of sediment.

1	Huang he ("Yellow River") (China)
2	Nile (Sudan/Egypt)
3	Ganges/Brahmaputra (India/Bangladesh)
4	Purari (Papua New Guinea)
5	Fly (Irian Jaya/Papua New Guinea)
6	Mississippi (U.S.)
7	Mekong (Cambodia/Vietnam)
8 (tie)	Po (Italy)
	Danube (Central/Eastern Europe)
10	Yukon (Alaska/Canada)

AQUATIC ANIMALS

Coastal waters around the world sustain a vast richness and range of life, from tiny microorganisms to great sea lions and sharks. The bigger animals depend on the smaller, with larger predators hunting and eating smaller species. They are all joined in a single elaborate food web.

A great white shark breaches to snatch a seal—which turns out to be a decoy.

LIGHT AND LIFE

The extraordinary profusion and diversity of life in coastal waters has several different causes: one is simply the shallowness of these seas. Beneath the open ocean the seabed lies in total darkness, but along the **continental shelf** (the area of shallow water near land), sunlight penetrates all the way down. Thus plants may find a firm hold in sand or rock, while still receiving light; shellfish and corals can cluster here as well. These provide food and hiding places for fish and crustaceans, such as crabs and lobsters.

PEOPLE FILE

CALYPSO MAN

No one did more to foster an understanding of the seas than the French diver Jacques Cousteau, whose films have thrilled and delighted millions all over the world. Traveling on his ship, the *Calypso*, he explored waters from the Great Barrier Reef to the Antarctic, and campaigned hard for the protection of threatened coastlines.

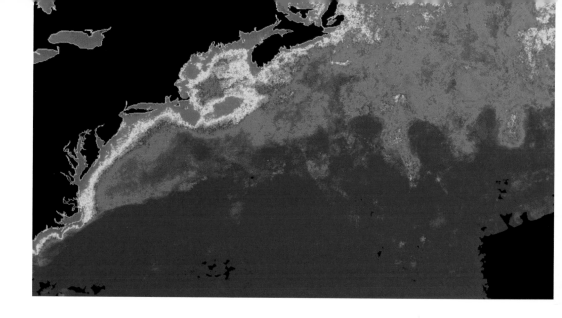

A satellite image reveals the distribution of phytoplankton in the western Atlantic. The richest areas (red) lie off the U.S. coast.

EAT AND BE EATEN

Another advantage of coastal waters over open sea is the richness of the nutrients—decayed animal or vegetable matter—brought down in river sediment. Similar nutrients build up on the seabeds of the deep oceans: along the western coasts of the great continents, these are brought up from the deeps by cold-water currents.

These nutrients feed the plankton that sit at the bottom of the food chain. Phytoplankton are microscopic plants; zooplankton are tiny animals: both are food for an amazing array of predators, from corals and crustaceans to tiny fish. These tiny fish are eaten by larger fish, which are snapped up in turn by sharks or marine mammals (small whales such as porpoises or dolphins, or shore-breeding species such as seals).

LOCATION FILE

COMBAT COAST

Each spring, more than 8,000 elephant seals come ashore to breed at Piedras Blancas, California. First, though, they must mate—which means the bulls (right) doing battle over females. Despite weighing a couple tons each, elephant seals get their name not from their size but from the trunk-like nose through which the aggressive bull makes his bellowing roar. It's such a spectacle that humans flock here almost as eagerly as the seals: more than 100,000 tourists come to Piedras Blancas every year.

Bull elephant seals battle for supremacy (and females) on the California coast.

A VARIETY OF BIRDS

Earth's coastal waters and beaches sustain an astonishing diversity of birds, from waders to mighty sea eagles, from gannets to scavenging gulls. Each species is superbly adapted to the food available to it: no food ever goes to waste along the coastlines.

SEABIRD CITIES

Vast colonies of seabirds nest on coastal cliffs around the world; others live on remote strips of coast and offshore islands. These seabird cities can be found from northern Scandinavia to southern Chile, from Canada to Australia and New Zealand. The colonies resemble human cities not only in their scale but in their social complexity. Tensions rise as birds try to live in such close quarters, not only with each other but with other species as well. Like cities, they have their seamy side: gangs of gulls that snatch unguarded eggs or abduct young fledglings; skuas that chase smaller fishing birds and terrify them into throwing up their hard-caught food.

This sheer cliff is home to a gravity-defying colony of kittiwakes.

A WORLD OF WADERS

Sandy beaches and mudflats have their own very different bird societies. Typical wading birds are long-legged to paddle through the shallows, and long-beaked to penetrate the sand for worms and tiny crustaceans. Waders often flock in the thousands, especially at **migration** time. Waders are often difficult to tell apart, since they are colored to fit in with the tawnies and golds of their sandy environment. But they have as many different designs of beak as a Swiss-Army knife has blades, according to whether they point, probe, dabble, flip pebbles, or skim the sand in their search for food.

A flock of lesser flamingos graces the coast of Namibia, at Walvis Bay. The cold waters here teem with the microorganisms on which flamingos feed.

A HOME FOR HUMANS

Coastal areas offer ready access to the resources of both sea and land, so it's no surprise that they should have appealed to the earliest humans. They were dependent on whatever food they could hunt near their homes, so it made sense for them to live near two potential sources of food: the land and the sea.

THE WORLD'S FIRST GARBAGE

The Klasies River Mouth, South Africa, is one of the most crucial archaeological sites in the world, though it has no great ruins, no precious jewelry, or princely tombs. Its main claims to fame are some bits of jawbone and the fact that it was a garbage dump. But the jawbone is recognizably human and 100,000 years old. This means the garbage is of considerable interest, for the details it can yield of the lifestyle of the first humans.

Harpoon at the ready, an Inuit hunts in Arctic waters.

A BALANCED DIET

There's no shortage of evidence—each generation added its waste until the accumulated pile was 66 feet (20 m) deep—and it makes clear that these communities looked both inland and out to sea for food. The shells of mussels and clams show that seafood figured in their diet, though the ancient people don't seem to have developed the skills or equipment for catching fish. There are bones, too: from penguins and seals, but also from antelope and even buffalo, killed on expeditions inland. People must have eaten roots, fruit, and herbs as well, though these don't leave the same lasting record.

THE SANDS OF TIME

Just north of Liverpool, England, Formby Beach has long been popular with joggers, dog-walkers, and day-trippers, all of whom leave their footprints in the sand. Now, however, a shift in tidal patterns has started to uncover traces left a lot longer ago: human and animal footprints, baked hard in the mud by the sun of 6,000 years ago, but till now covered over with softer sand, have started to appear.

PEOPLE FILE

WASHED UP

In 1805, the Lewis and Clark expedition across North America reached the Pacific after an epic trek over the Rockies. Kallamuck Indians offered them blubber from the carcass of a stranded whale: "I had a part of it cooked and found it very palatable and tender," wrote Captain Lewis.

Above: Istanbul's position on the busy waterways of the Bosporus has made it a major trading center for many centuries.

COASTAL MANAGEMENT

T he sea is a formidable enemy; over time, coastal flooding has claimed countless lives and large areas of what might have been useful land. Humans have not been content simply to submit to the will of the waves, but have tried to hold the sea back by means of coastal defenses.

Some 70 percent of the world's sandy beaches are now suffering significant erosion. If the problem becomes worse, it seems likely that it will spell disaster for many tourist-dependent local economies. Even so, such difficulties are less dramatic than those faced by many cliff-top communities worldwide, who see their homes threatened by erosion.

BEATING A RETREAT

The sea creates as much new land through deposition as it destroys by coastal erosion, but this is of little consolation to those whose homes are built on eroding land. Despite this, many experts now argue that the most sensible approach is simply to allow the sea to break down the land in some places and then build it up in others.

FACT FILE

COASTLINE DEFENSES (AND THEIR DRAWBACKS)
• SEA WALLS Made of concrete; effective, but enormously expensive both to build and maintain.
• GROINS Low walls extending outward at right angles to the shoreline, to keep the beach from being carried away by longshore drift.
• GABIONS Wire-net bales packed with chunks of rock; effective, but expensive, and ugly to look at.
• REVETMENTS Low wooden barriers running parallel to a beach or cliff-base; unsightly, and easily damaged.

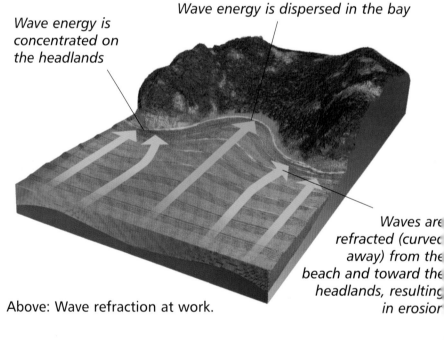

Wave energy is concentrated on the headlands

Wave energy is dispersed in the bay

Waves are refracted (curved away) from the beach and toward the headlands, resulting in erosion

Above: Wave refraction at work.

A homeowner looks on helplessly as seawater surges into his living room: for many, the sea is too close a neighbor for comfort.

A marina at Chestertown, Maryland, in the aftermath of Hurricane Frederick, 1979.

MAKING A STAND

Sometimes—where whole towns or important roads are threatened, for example—the sea has to be held back. One way of doing this is through beach replenishment (the replacement of eroded material with imported sand or stone). Another is the construction of sea walls, though these are very expensive.

Artificial reefs set some distance offshore may offer a compromise solution. Although a firm concrete base is needed, these barriers can be built from waste tires or other ballast—they don't have to be completely impenetrable, just to interrupt the rhythm of the waves, sapping some of their energy. Other solutions have included artificial islands and breakwaters standing at right-angles out from the shore: these, too, help break up the rhythm of the advancing waves. The key problem—apart from the cost—is that a measure that successfully stops erosion at one point on the coast often makes it worse at another.

LOCATION FILE

NARROWNECK—MAKING WAVES

The beach at Gold Coast, Queensland, Australia, has been badly eroded over the years—a threat not only to the local tourist-trade but to those parts of the city facing flooding. Now an artificial reef, known as Narrowneck, or Nazz, built from sandbags 492 feet (150 m) offshore, is helping to protect the sands onshore. At the same time, though, by directing the swell more precisely, it's producing bigger and better waves for the surfers now flocking to Gold Coast in ever-increasing numbers.

THE KINDLY COAST

Rugged mountains, scorching deserts, or dense forests occupy the interiors of many countries, making coastal areas the only parts that are readily habitable for humans. Low-lying, cooled by breezes, and furnished with relatively rich soils, the coastal strip is often the place in which it's easiest to live.

THE FIRST AUSTRALIANS

When the first Aborigines came to Australia, some 70,000 years ago, they arrived by crossing the Timor Sea or the Torres Strait. While their first settlements were along the northern coast, over generations they expanded farther and farther inland. They found ways of living off the land without harming it, and could survive in the harshest environments.

Agriculture in Algeria relies heavily on irrigation channels like the one visible on the right of this field.

LOCATION FILE

ALGERIA

More than 80 percent of Algeria lies in the Sahara Desert; much of what remains is covered by the rugged Atlas Mountains. In all, only six percent of the country's land area is suitable for agriculture: most of this can be found along the Mediterranean coast in a strip just 12 to 50 miles (20–80 km) wide. Here, in temperatures moderated by sea breezes, and in fertile soils, are the fields where Algeria's farmers grow wheat, dates, olives, and citrus fruits, and keep herds of dairy cattle.

Sydney's northern suburbs hug the coast: like most Australians, the inhabitants live within a short distance of the shore.

THROUGH EUROPEAN EYES

The first European settlers in Australia had a very different attitude toward land use. The Aborigines were grateful for whatever the land provided, but the newcomers were farmers, who felt the country should be put to work. Any land not suitable for this approach was described as "waste," making the Australian interior not only dangerous but also useless. The new arrivals valued the land along the coast for its gentle gradients, its cooling breezes, and its fertile soils. Although the expansion in sheep ranching significantly extended the productive area into the hills inland, vast areas of the continent are still unused. Industry needed reliable water supplies, level sites, and convenient access, which were all found on the coast. It was also far easier to build roads and railways along the coastal plains.

LOCATION FILE

THE ATACAMA DESERT

The world's driest desert lies right beside its biggest ocean: the Atacama runs the length of Chile, between the Pacific and the Andes. On average, it rains once a century here, but some areas claim not to have seen a shower in 400 years. This coastal area is in the rain shadow of the Andes—most rain falls on the eastern side of the mountains.

TRADE

A country's coasts are vital in offering access to a wider world: trade brings not only prosperity but also understanding of other peoples. For centuries, the sea was the only realistic route for large-scale commerce. Even now, huge amounts of goods are shipped around the world each year.

GLOBAL SHIPPING INDUSTRY

Once, those who wished to trade across the seas had no alternative but to go by ship; today, goods —like people—can be whisked around the globe by air. Even so, for products where delivery is not urgent, transport by sea is far cheaper than by air.

Ships still trade back and forth across the world's oceans, moving the goods on which the world economy depends. Refrigerated ships bring meat, fruit, and vegetables, and dry bulk carriers carry grain—or a range of other cargoes from coal to metal ore. Giant supertankers bring petroleum, and smaller vessels carry other oils, from soybean to olive. There are even ships that specialize in transporting wine.

New York City: America's northern Atlantic gateway for 200 hectic years, New York saw the arrival of generations of European immigrants by boat.

Vast numbers of containers are stacked up on docks, crossing the oceans or being transported aboard trucks every moment of every day.

INTERMODAL SHIPPING

The last three decades have seen the growth of what is known as intermodal shipping: goods are packed in metal containers that can be transferred quickly and easily from one form of transportation to another. A container originating in a factory in Koln, Germany, for example, may be loaded onto a truck, train, or barge for the journey to Rotterdam. There it may be lifted onto the deck of a specially designed container ship. On arrival at its destination port, it can easily be transferred to another truck, train, or boat for final delivery. In this way, a single shipment is passed easily from one form of transportation to another.

For short sea-crossings, ro-ro (roll-on, roll-off) ferries allow laden trucks simply to drive aboard in one port, and drive ashore again at another.

 FACT FILE

TOP 10 WORLD PORTS
(by tonnage of shipping handled, 2000)

1   Singapore
2   Hong Kong (China)
3   Rotterdam (Netherlands)
4   Kaohsiung (Taiwan)
5   Los Angeles/Long Beach (U.S.)
6   Busan (South Korea)
7   New Orleans (U.S.)
8   Houston (U.S.)
9   Antwerp (Belgium)
10   Nagoya (Japan)

COASTAL NAVIGATION

1f the ports along the coastlines are essential gateways to shipping, other stretches of coast may be fearful hazards. Great effort and ingenuity has gone into keeping channels open and clearly marked. Even so, there are still shipwrecks from time to time.

LIGHTHOUSES

Greek legend tells of coastal beacons lit to guide the conquering heroes home from Troy; the great Pharos, the lighthouse at Alexandria, Egypt, was one of the wonders of the ancient world. But things have moved on. Lighthouses now use the latest lightbulbs and reflective mirrors of complex, computerized design. A modern light can be clearly visible miles away, in any weather. With radar detection and radio-links, moreover, lighthouse-keepers and coastguards can anticipate trouble before it happens, and communicate with vessels that appear to wander off-course.

Today's satellite navigation systems allow a ship's crew to pinpoint their whereabouts to within a few yards, while sonar echo-sounding lets them look out for unexpected shallows. The captains of coastal ships still need to be able to read a well-made and updated chart that shows the whereabouts of concealed rocks or (often shifting) sandbanks. They are helped by buoys anchored to the seabed, which float on the surface, marking the channel.

LOCATION FILE

THE ANYTHING-BUT-LIGHT HOUSE

Built in the 1870s, and with a height of more than 200 feet (60 m), the world's tallest brick lighthouse, North Carolina's Cape Hatteras Lighthouse, weighs in at well over 4,400 tons (4,000 t). Yet the lighthouse was built on a foundation of sand—which was steadily being eroded by Atlantic waves. In 1999, a team of engineers set to work, jacking the entire structure up on 100 hydraulic jacks. Using a specially designed steel track, they moved it to another site almost a mile away on higher ground. The lighthouse is out of reach of the ocean's destructive force—for now, at least.

Coastal trade is the economic lifeblood of settlements up and down Brazil's Atlantic seaboard.

Even with today's technology to help, sea captains still need to be able to read a chart. Here, a navigator plots his vessel's course through coastal waters.

DREDGING

Natural channels may need to be widened and deepened by dredgers—vessels specially equipped to scoop away at the seabed, removing vast quantities of mud and sand. There are two main types of dredgers. The dipper dredge shovels up material from the bottom like a digger. Hydraulic dredges operate more like underwater vacuum cleaners. Today's supertankers and container ships often have deep **draughts** and need plenty of clearance if they're not to run aground.

FACT FILE

HISTORIC SHIPWRECKS

• c. 1300 B.C. A Syrian trader wrecked off Cape Gelidonya, southern Turkey.

• c. 400 B.C. The Kyrenia Ship, a Greek cargo vessel, sank off Kyrenia, Cyprus.

• c. 80 B.C. Roman cargo ship sank off the island of Antikythera, southern Greece, carrying a remarkable mechanism believed by many to have been an early computer.

• A.D. 1545 Henry VIII's warship, the *Mary Rose*, sank off southern England.

• 1622 An entire Spanish treasure fleet was wrecked in the Straits of Florida.

FISHING

T hroughout history, the sea has been a great storehouse of food for humans. Fishing has been a vital activity for coast-dwelling peoples through thousands of years. Fishing today is a modern industry, with high-tech trawlers and giant factory-ships. Nonetheless, there are still small-scale fishermen in many countries.

LOCATION FILE

THE DIVERS OF CHEJU

For more than 1,500 years, the (traditionally female) *haenyo* divers of Cheju, South Korea, have plunged to depths of up to 82 feet (25 m) for minutes at a time in search of the shellfish for which the island is renowned. But times have changed, and with them Korea's economic fortunes, leaving few prepared to undertake such dangerous and grueling work. In the 1930s, there were more than 20,000 *haenyo*; today, there are only 3,000—and most of them are in their 50s and 60s.

A LIVING FROM THE SEA

Every morning for thousands of years, fishermen have set out from the Yemeni coast, their streamlined sambouks taking the breakers of the Indian Ocean in their stride. Today, though, Yemen's traditional fishermen are forced to compete for fast-dwindling stocks of fish with fleets of foreign trawlers and giant factory-ships operating offshore.

Right: Modern methods have allowed vast numbers of fish to be caught, but there are already signs that humans may be exhausting this precious resource.

Below: A Burmese fisherman works the traditional way, catching enough for his family—and a little extra to trade.

The three main fishing nets used today.

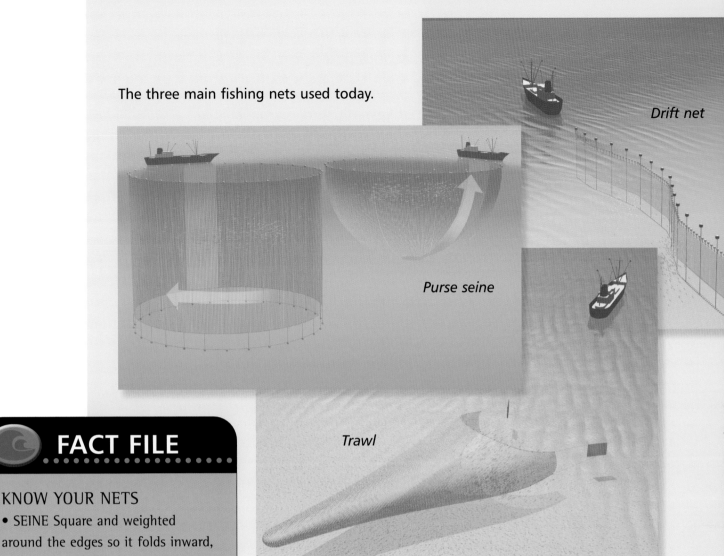

Drift net

Purse seine

Trawl

FACT FILE

KNOW YOUR NETS

• SEINE Square and weighted around the edges so it folds inward, enveloping fish. Thrown by hand, it is the essential tool of the traditional fisherman.
• PURSE SEINE A seine net large enough to catch an entire shoal of fish, and big enough to hold St. Paul's Cathedral in London, UK.
• TRAWL A big bag held open at the mouth, and drawn behind a boat. Some trawls today have an opening that could admit a dozen jumbo jets!
• DRIFT Widely banned, yet still much used, drift nets are weighted at the bottom but buoyed up at the top with floats to form a mesh wall that may extend more than six miles (10 km).

AN INCREASING CATCH

Fishing is an industry now, with huge catches and financial fortunes to be made. Fish are not just a food for humans, but a basis for livestock feed. Fifty years ago, the total world catch was just under 22 million tons (20 million t) per year; by 1990, it was well over four times that figure.

Such catches can't be sustained. Already, Canada has had to close the once-rich Newfoundland cod fisheries in an effort to preserve the small remaining stocks of fish. Similar measures are being contemplated for the North Sea, while western Atlantic tuna catches are 1/12th what they were a generation ago. In wealthy countries, the costs of the collapse in fishing have been fearful, with many people losing their jobs. Poorer countries stand to lose much more—for 40 percent of the world's population, fish is the primary source of protein.

SEASIDE TOURISM

Today, many people spend at least one vacation a year at the beach. Many others visit the seaside for a weekend, or even just for a day trip when they have some time off work. But the idea of taking a vacation at the seaside is a comparatively recent one.

GROWTH OF SEASIDE VACATIONS

The association of the coast with health and recreation is very much a product of the industrial age. Only when people began working in factories and offices did seaside vacations start to become popular. The construction of the first railways in the 19th century helped, making travel to the coast possible for the first time for many people. With money to spend and regular time off, thousands flocked to the new seaside resorts.

In the 20th century, the number of cars on the road began to increase. Cars were sometimes advertised as a means of escape—often escape to the seaside.

Hotels and villas crowd behind a beach swarming with vacationers: an everyday scene in popular tourist resorts around the world.

PEOPLE FILE

THOMAS COOK
Born in the English Midlands, Thomas Cook grew up a Baptist missionary, promoting the ways of godliness and temperance (abstention from alcohol). It was for a temperance meeting that, in 1841, he organized his first railway excursion, chartering a train from Leicester to nearby Loughborough. Over the next 10 years, he arranged more trips, building up the world's first travel agency. By 1856, he was offering European tours.

THE ANNUAL MIGRATION

Air travel extended everyone's range: by the 1960s, northern European vacationers were flying south to the Spanish *Costas* ("coast"), drawn by cheap prices and guaranteed sunshine. With everything included, from hotel to entertainment, the **package tour** took all the complications out of foreign travel.

TAILOR-MADE TOURISM

Over time, people began to feel they were themselves being "packaged" by their vacations, crammed by the thousands into identical hotels in identical resorts. Some people began demanding more personalized treatment, with everything from whale-watching and cultural visits to jet-skiing and scuba-diving. A new breed of young backpacking tourists traveled farther afield in search of relaxation and fun, exploring coasts from Brazil to Bali, from South Africa to Thailand.

A Filipino fishing community celebrates the whale shark, their economic mainstay—once they hunted these giant, harmless sharks, now they act as guides for tourists.

A FRAGILE ENVIRONMENT

The coasts are often extraordinarily beautiful and rich in wildlife of every kind, but they are also environments of great sensitivity. Today, the coastlines of the world are subject to many pressures, including the construction of homes and businesses, watersports activities, and the pumping of untreated sewage.

DEVELOPMENT OR DAMAGE?

Countless miles of coastline around the world have been covered over by developments of high-rise hotels and resorts. Whether one visits the Seychelles; Acapulco, Mexico; or the Red Sea coast of Egypt, these large tourist resorts tend to look much like each other. Although this kind of development can bring jobs and money to the area, sand dunes, salt marshes, coral reefs, and mangrove swamps are all destroyed to pay for this economic growth.

Container-ports, highways, apartment buildings, golf courses, theme parks, and a variety of other developments also affect coastlines around the world. Some areas are now protected. For example, measures passed as a result of the California Coastal Act of 1976 have severely restricted the development of sensitive seacoast areas in that state, whether for tourism or other uses.

FACT FILE

SOURCES OF SEA POLLUTION
- DIRECT DISCHARGE Sewage and industrial effluents (waste products) are often pumped straight into the sea.
- LAND RUNOFF Agricultural chemicals (fertilizers, weedkillers, etc.) are washed into streams and rivers by rain, then carried down to the sea.
- ATMOSPHERIC FALLOUT Airborne pollution, in smoke or fumes, is washed down into the sea by rainfall.

A beautiful golf course—but was it built in a coastal habitat that was once home to animals and birds?

POLLUTION

In the developed world today, factories rarely belch out smoke or pour foul-smelling sludge into the ocean around the clock, as they used to do in the past. But some firms have been caught causing pollution, and accidents can happen even in well-run factories. This is a real problem where, as in the nuclear and chemical industries, even a relatively small accidental discharge can have disastrous consequences for the environment and public health.

Developing countries desperate to improve their standard of living may feel that strict regulation is a luxury they can't afford. They also point out that the world's wealthiest countries often got rich by polluting their environments. In some cases, big companies from the developed world have used poorer countries as dumping-grounds for hazardous chemicals.

Above: **Coastal development can be a form of pollution. This stretch of coastline, for example, has been thoroughly concreted over.**

LOCATION FILE

GALICIA

When an aging oil tanker, the *Prestige*, sank off Galicia, Spain, in November 2002, a third of the 66,000 tons (60,000 t) of crude oil it was carrying leaked out. Oil covered several hundred miles of coastline, overwhelming tourist beaches and seabird colonies and destroying 21,500 jobs in Galicia's important fishing industry. The bulk of the tanker's cargo sank with it to the bottom, but hopes that the low temperatures there would cause it to congeal safely have proved unfounded. The *Prestige* disaster may still be in its early days.

Volunteers help clear up the mess left on the Galician coast by the *Prestige* disaster.

43

A WORLD AWASH?

S ome change in sea level over time is natural, but recently, people have become concerned that human pollution is responsible for global warming, causing sea levels to rise. If they do rise significantly, many coastal areas could be at risk, with potentially disastrous consequences.

GLOBAL WARMING?

Sea levels have risen and fallen significantly throughout Earth's history. Therefore, it should not be assumed that the current coastlines will be there forever. If fears of global warming are correct, then they are already changing. The cause is the greenhouse effect, by which carbon dioxide (CO_2) and water vapor in Earth's atmosphere trap heat from the sun that might otherwise escape into space. This effect is in itself perfectly natural and even helpful. Without it, the ice age would have continued more or less indefinitely; Earth's mean surface temperature would be between 5 and -13 °F (–15 and –25 °C), rather than its present 59 °F (15 °C). The problem is that, thanks to pollution from industry, aircraft, and motor vehicles, the last century has seen an unprecedented accumulation of **greenhouse gases**—leading, say many scientists, to global warming. Since warmer water takes up more space, its molecules expanding, sea levels will inevitably rise as Earth's temperature does.

However, not everyone agrees that sea level rises will have a dramatic effect. The Intergovernmental Panel on Climate Change forecasts a change in sea level over the following 110 years of up to .03 inches (0.77 mm) per year. Some climatologists now say that that number is highly unlikely, and that the actual change will be far less.

THE MARSHALL ISLANDS

Of the 34 islands that make up the Marshall group, few rise much more than eight feet (2.5 m) above the surrounding Pacific Ocean at their highest points. Should sea levels rise by 1.6 feet (0.5 m), as they easily could over the coming decades, life for the islanders would be badly affected. The problem is not that entire islands would be submerged, but that the normal storm-surges and high tides might do much more damage to precious agricultural land and freshwater supplies. A series of severe floods has already forced islanders in some places to leave their homes for higher ground, at least for a time: many face the real prospect of becoming permanent environmental refugees.

A California farm lies largely submerged in floodwater.

Above: Even airborne toxins are eventually carried to the sea by rainfall and rivers.

Right: A Shanghai factory belches out pollutants.

AHEAD OF HIS TIME: JEAN BAPTISTE FOURIER

The idea of the greenhouse effect is nothing new: Jean Baptiste Fourier, the man who first proposed it, was born in France in 1768, and set out his theory in 1827. Although celebrated in his day—and for generations after—for his work as a pioneering mathematician, the importance of his thoughts on the heat-retaining properties of Earth's atmosphere have only just begun to be appreciated.

GLOSSARY

Continental shelf The relatively shallow stretch of sea extending out from the coasts of any continent, before the bottom falls away and the deep sea starts.

Convection (overturn) Convection is that process by which, when air or water is warmed, it expands and becomes less dense, rising as a result, and allowing cooler, denser air or water to sink beneath it and push it upward. Over time, a continuous circulation or convective overturn may be established.

Coriolis effect The apparent effect of Earth's spin on objects that move across its surface. For example, though a current may want to head straight north, it cannot: Earth spins westward beneath it, meaning that the current bends away to the east.

Cyclones Spiraling currents of air produced where a small area of ocean surface heats up quickly and the air above it rises; this can often lead to violent storms.

Draughts The depths of loaded ships in the water, measured from the waterline to the lowest point on a ship's hull.

Ecosystem A clearly defined area in which the living organisms react with each other and with their chemical and physical environment to form a stable system.

Equatorial To do with the equator, an imaginary line drawn around Earth at its widest point, farthest from the poles.

Food web A series of organisms related by the fact that each feeds on its predecessor in the chain: e.g., plant, herbivore, carnivore.

Glaciations The processes by which much of the planet becomes covered in deep ice sheets; the period in which this happens is also known as an ice age.

Gravitational force The attraction exerted by any object; Earth's gravity is what gives people weight and stops them from floating off the ground.

Greenhouse gases Those gases (such as carbon dioxide, water vapor, or methane) which increase the tendency of the atmosphere to retain heat from the sun.

Hominids Human ancestors, or modern humans; many scientists also say that chimpanzees and gorillas should be considered hominids.

Homo sapiens The Latin name for the human being in its fully developed form.

Hydraulic To do with water, especially the behavior of water under pressure or in confined spaces.

Latitudes Distance north or south of the equator, measured in degrees (°) from the center of Earth to its surface.

Magma The deep layer of super-hot rock that underlies Earth's solid crust; when it seeps out to the surface in liquid form it is known as lava.

Mangrove A tree that grows along tropical coasts with its roots anchored in mud, but with pores above the surface through which they are supplied with air. Mangroves form forests that trap mud, thereby extending the coastline, and provide a sheltered habitat for many animals. There are several species of mangrove.

Microorganisms Microscopic life-forms; plants or animals that are too tiny to see with the naked eye.

Migration The movement of a population of animals or people from one place to another. Many bird species migrate long distances every year.

Mollusks Invertebrate animals belonging to a group of more than 80,000 species, most of which live in water. Many secrete an external shell or have internal shells that serve as skeletons. The group includes clams, oysters, mussels, snails, slugs, octopuses, and squid.

Package tour A vacation in which transportation, accommodation, and possibly entertainment and outings are bought together in a single "package."

Plates Vast slabs of rock, floating on magma, of which Earth's surface is comprised.

Sediment Any undissolved matter carried by a liquid; the sand or mud a flowing river sweeps down to the sea; different rivers have different sediment-loads depending on the sort of rocks they have to traverse on their way to the sea.

Seismic Relating to earthquakes.

Transmission The passing-on of something.

FURTHER INFORMATION

WEB SITES TO VISIT

http://www.greenpeace.org

The site of the environmental activists' organization Greenpeace International, whose campaigns cover every aspect of the environment, including coastlines.
Greenpeace USA
702 H Street NW
Suite 300
Washington, D.C. 20001
Tel: (202) 462-1177
Fax: (202) 462-4507
E-mail: greenpeace.usa@wdc.greenpeace.org

http://www.panda.org

The site of WWF, the global environment network.
WWF-United States
1250 24th Street NW
Washington, D.C. 20037-1175
Tel: (202) 293-9211
Fax: (202) 293-4800

http://www.nationalgeographic.com

The site of the National Geographic Society offers invaluable maps and stunning photos.
National Geographic Society
1145 17th Street NW
Washington, D.C. 20036-4688
Tel: (800) 647-5463
E-mail: askngs@nationalgeographic.com

BOOKS TO READ

Hirschi, Ron, and Peggy Bauer. *Save Our Oceans and Coasts*. New York: Dell Publishing, 1993.

Massa, Renato. *Along the Coasts*. Austin, Tex.: Raintree Steck-Vaughn, 1997.

Mudd-Ruth, Maria. *Pacific Coast*. New York: Marshall Cavendish, 2000.

Pringle, Laurence. *Global Warming: The Threat of Earth's Changing Climate*. New York: North-South Books, 2003.

INDEX

agriculture 32, 42, 45
Antarctic Current 13
archaeological sites 28

bars 20, 21
bays 19, 30
beaches 16, 17
    erosion 18, 31
    tourism 40
    wading birds 27
birds 5, 22, 26–27, 46
    tourism 42
buoys 36

caves 19
cliffs 18, 26
climate 7, 13, 14
coastal defenses 30–31
continental shelf 24, 46
convection currents 14, 15, 46
coral reef 5, 21, 24, 25, 42
Coriolis effect 12, 46
Cousteau, Jacques 24
currents 12–13, 20, 25, 46
cyclones 15, 46

deltas 22–23
deposition 20–21, 30

earthquakes 4, 6, 8, 9
ecology 12, 13, 23
ecosystems 5, 22, 46
energy 12, 15
    waves 8, 9, 18, 30, 31
equatorial currents 12, 13
erosion 18–19, 20, 30, 31
estuaries 22

fish 21, 22, 24, 25, 27
fishing 17, 38–39, 43
flooding 30, 31, 45
food chains & webs 24, 25, 46

glaciation 6, 7, 46
global warming 44
gravity 17, 22, 46
    tides 10, 11
Great Barrier Reef 21
Great Conveyor Current 13
greenhouse effect 44, 45, 46
Gulf Stream 12, 13

headlands 18, 19, 30
hurricanes 8, 15, 31

industry 33
    fishing 38, 39, 43
    pollution 5, 42, 43, 44
    shipping 34
    tourism 41

lighthouses 36
longshore drift 16, 17, 20, 30

mammals 5, 25
mangroves 4, 22, 27, 42, 46
mollusks 5, 6, 21, 46
mudflats 22, 27

navigation 36–37
nutrients 12, 22, 25

pebbles 16, 17, 18, 20
plankton 25
pollution 5, 42, 43, 44, 45
ports 35, 36, 42

rivers 4, 20, 22, 23, 25, 46
rocky shores 8, 19

salt marshes 4, 21, 22–23, 42
sand 16, 18, 20, 29, 46
sand dunes 4, 17, 42
sandy beaches 8, 16, 27, 30
satellite navigation 36

scuba diving 41
sea level changes 7, 44–45
sea walls 30, 31
seabirds 26, 43
seashells 16
seashore 16–17
seaside 40
seaweeds 5
sediment 4, 17, 23, 25, 46
sewage 5, 42
sharks 24, 25, 41
shellfish 24, 28
ships 34, 36, 37
    fishing 38
    navigation 36
    trade 34, 35
spits 20, 21
stacks 18, 19
storms 15, 18, 46
surfing 15, 31

tides 4, 10–11, 22
tourism 25, 40–41, 42, 43
    coastal defenses 30, 31
trade 5, 29, 34–35, 36, 38
tropical storms 15
tsunamis 8, 9

volcanoes 4, 6, 9, 16

wading birds 26, 27
water sports 42
water temperature 13, 14
wave refraction 9, 19, 30
waves 4, 8–9, 15
    erosion 16, 17, 18, 19, 30, 31
weather 12, 14–15
whale-watching 41
winds 4, 8, 14, 15
    currents 12, 13